Peyton MANNING

By Jim Gigliotti

The
**Child's
World**
www.childsworld.com

J
B
MANNING
Pe.

Published in the United States of America by The Child's World®
P.O. Box 326 • Chanhassen, MN 55317-0326
800-599-READ • www.childsworld.com

ACKNOWLEDGMENTS

The Child's World®: Mary Berendes, Publishing Director

Produced by Shoreline Publishing Group LLC
President / Editorial Director: James Buckley, Jr.
Designer: Tom Carling, carlingdesign.com
Assistant Editor: Ellen Labrecque

Photo Credits
Cover: Joe Robbins
Interior: Corbis: 1; Getty Images: 7, 10, 12, 13, 15, 17, 18, 19, 22, 26;
Joe Robbins: 3, 5, 20, 25, 28

LIBRARY OF CONGRESS
CATALOGING-IN-PUBLICATION DATA

Gigliotti, Jim.
  Peyton Manning / by Jim Gigliotti.
     p. cm. — (The world's greatest athletes)
  Includes bibliographical references and index.
  ISBN 1-59296-758-2 (library bound : alk. paper)
  1. Manning, Peyton—Juvenile literature. 2. Football players—
United States—Biography—Juvenile literature. I. Title. II. Series.
  GV939.M289G54 2006
  796.332092—dc22
                                        2006006291

CONTENTS

Calling the Signals to Win

PEYTON MANNING APPROACHES THE LINE OF scrimmage, and the routine begins. Peyton, the star quarterback of the Indianapolis Colts, starts pointing fingers and making hand gestures. He hollers commands at his teammates. Check that weakside linebacker! The cornerback is coming on a blitz! You need to block that defensive end!

Some of the two-time NFL most valuable player's actions are just for show. Sometimes, Peyton is just trying to confuse and distract the opposition. But most times, he's **exhorting** and instructing his fellow members of the Colts' offense. And on many occasions, he is also changing the play that was sent in from the sidelines by the coaches. The Colts have that much confidence in him!

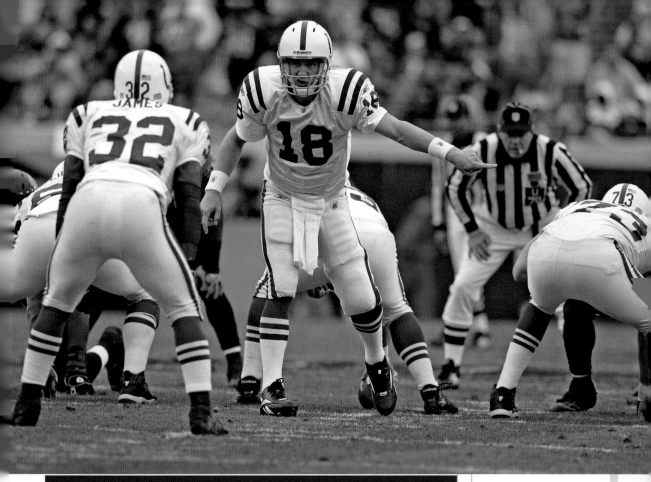

Few NFL quarterbacks have the freedom that Manning has to change the play at the line of scrimmage.

Whatever he is doing on a particular play, though, Peyton approaches his pre-snap routine like an active orchestra conductor. Peyton conducted the Colts' offense to an NFL-best 14-2 record in 2005.

Plus, the Colts have been among the league's best offenses in the early 2000s. There's no doubt that the man in charge of that point-scoring machine is Peyton Manning, the quarterback from the South who was born to be a leader.

CHAPTER 1

Born to Be a Quarterback

PEYTON MANNING WAS BORN IN NEW ORLEANS, Louisiana, on March 24, 1976. His dad, Archie Manning, was the quarterback of the New Orleans Saints at the time. But Archie didn't try to raise Peyton to be an NFL quarterback just because he was one himself.

Sure, they played catch in the backyard, but Archie never pressured Peyton, older brother Cooper, or younger brother Eli (who became the quarterback of the New York Giants) to follow in his footsteps. In fact, Peyton wasn't even allowed to play organized football until seventh grade. He mostly played baseball.

Still, Peyton learned a lot by watching his dad— and not just about playing quarterback, either. He saw how his father handled the pressure and the

Though he was beloved in New Orleans, Archie Manning could never lead the Saints to a winning season.

responsibilities—even when he was off the field. Archie was one of the most famous people in New Orleans, and everywhere he went people wanted to say hello or ask for an autograph. Sometimes, they approached Archie when he was having dinner out with Peyton and the rest of the family.

Peyton watched as his father handled every situation with class and dignity. Archie knew it was important that he give back to the community that had given him so much support. He always had a

A trio of Manning QBs: Archie (left) is the only person to have two sons, Eli (center) and Peyton, follow him to the NFL.

Young Peyton Manning

- Lived in the famous Garden District in New Orleans, near neighbors such as novelist Anne Rice and musician Trent Reznor (of Nine Inch Nails)

- Learned about quarterbacking by sitting in on team meetings as a youngster when his dad, Archie, played for the New Orleans Saints

- Originally played wide receiver in high school, catching passes from older brother Cooper, who was the school's quarterback

- Was named the Gatorade Circle of Champions National Player of the Year for the 1993 season while at Isidore Newman High School in New Orleans, Louisiana

kind word and a smile on his face for his fans, and helped with as many charity requests as he could.

"My father has always been my role model, both as a person and as a quarterback," Peyton said before he was drafted by the Colts in 1998. "If I could play as long as my father did in the NFL and also handle the things the way he handled them, that would be a real achievement for me."

Anyone who has watched Peyton conduct himself since joining Indianapolis in 1998 would agree that it's mission accomplished.

Peyton's decision to attend Tennesse shocked many people. His success there showed that he had made the right choice.

CHAPTER 2

A Victorious Volunteer

WHILE IN HIGH SCHOOL IN NEW ORLEANS IN THE early 1990s, Peyton helped Isidore Newman High win 34 of 39 games in three seasons. By the time he was a senior in 1993, he was the most highly recruited quarterback in the nation. Dozens of colleges wanted him to come to their school.

Archie Manning had been a legend at the University of Mississippi (also called "Ole Miss"). Many of that school's fans thought they'd soon have another Manning in their lineup. But Peyton wanted to create his own identity. When it came time for him to pick a college, he chose the University of Tennessee—one of Ole Miss' rivals—instead.

Followers of the Volunteers (as Tennessee teams are known) were **ecstatic**. Head coach Phillip Fulmer couldn't wait to see his prized recruit take the field.

Peyton lived up to the **hype**. He took over as the Volunteers' starting quarterback in his fourth game—and stayed there the rest of his career. By the time he finished his four years at Tennessee, Peyton had passed for more yards (11,201) and more touchdowns (89) than any other quarterback in school history. In all, he set 33 school records while leading the Volunteers to 39 wins in his 45 games as their starting quarterback.

Peyton was a standout in the classroom, too. He was an Academic All-American, and he graduated *cum laude* [koom LOW-day] with a degree in speech communication in only three years. Whether he had graduated or not, he could have skipped his final season of **eligibility** in 1997 and gone on to the NFL. He would almost certainly have been the first player chosen that year. His contract would have been worth several millions of dollars. Almost everyone urged him to leave college and go pro.

In making his decision, Peyton showed again that he was his own man. He enjoyed the college atmosphere so much that he decided that he wanted to come back to play one more season. "My college

Athletes in college normally get four years of eligibility. In recent years, more and more players have been choosing to leave school early to turn pro.

experience was a really good one, so I decided to stay all four years," Peyton says.

Peyton's senior season turned out to be a memorable one. He set school records by passing for 3,819 yards and 36 touchdowns while leading the Volunteers to 11 victories and the Southeastern Conference championship. He was the runner-up in the voting for the Heisman Trophy as college football's best player (finishing second to Charles

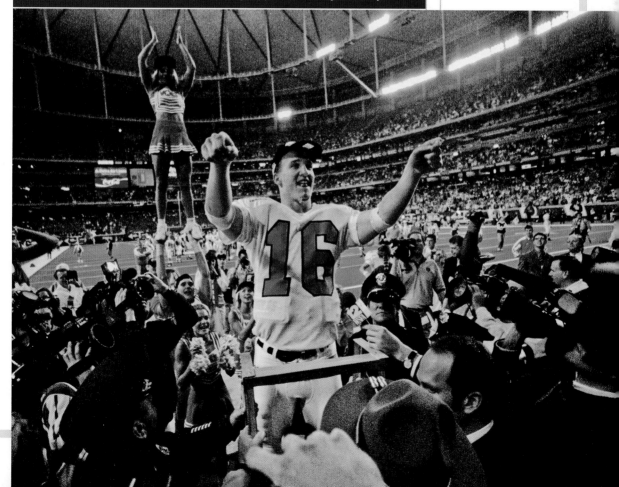

Big man on campus: After a Tennessee win, Peyton conducts the school band in playing "Rocky Top," their fight song.

Woodson of Michigan), and he won the prestigious Sullivan Award as the top **amateur** athlete in the United States.

And in the end, Peyton got his big contract, anyway. He was the first player selected in the NFL draft in the spring of 1998, and he signed a multi-year contract with the Indianapolis Colts.

Another Manning was on his way to becoming a top NFL quarterback.

Tennessee coach Philip Fulmer loved having the smart, strong-armed Peyton on his team for four seasons.

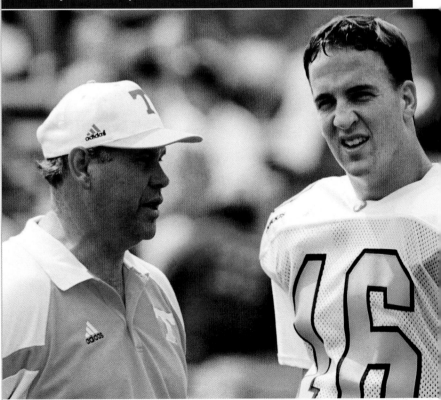

In His Own Words

Peyton Manning, on staying in school for his final year instead of joining the NFL and signing a big contract. Peyton says on his Web site, peytonmanning.com. :

"I didn't want to look back and say I wish I would have stayed my senior year. That's really what it was in a nutshell. I just kind of wanted to be a senior in college. I had already completed my degree in three years, so I knew I had a chance to slow things down a little bit. I had the opportunity to really take everything in and create a lot of memories for myself, and I'm certainly glad I did...I just wanted to enjoy being a college senior. For some reason, people had a really hard time believing that."

CHAPTER 3

A Perfectly Pure Passer

IT WAS CLEAR FROM THE START IN 1998 THAT THE Indianapolis Colts had a future superstar quarterback on their roster. In fact, the very first time that Peyton Manning dropped back to pass in an NFL game, he completed a 48-yard touchdown strike to wide receiver Marvin Harrison in a preseason contest against the Seattle Seahawks.

"He's going to be one of the special ones," New England cornerback Ty Law predicted after facing Peyton in two games in the quarterback's rookie season.

Peyton was the number-one draft pick in 1998, and it's hard to believe now that there was any debate over the choice. At the time, though, football experts were divided over whether Manning or Ryan

The Colts hoped that by drafting Peyton as the number-one overall pick, he would them into a winning team.

Leaf of Washington State would make a better player in the NFL.

Leaf, who was chosen by the San Diego Chargers with the second pick but played only a few years in the league, may have been the better pure athlete. But the Colts felt that Peyton's dedication, hard work, and intelligence made him the better fit—and they were right.

Peyton passed for 302 yards in his first regular-season game as a rookie for the Colts in 1998, but Indianapolis lost to Miami 24–15. That was about how it went in his first NFL season. Peyton passed for lots of yards (3,739) and touchdowns (26), but there were lots of losses, too (the Colts dropped 13 of 16 games).

The question of Leaf (left) or Manning raged before the 1998 NFL draft.

Still, Indianapolis saw enough to know that they had a future superstar in their lineup. For his part, Peyton set out to make sure that the team's losing ways would quickly become a thing of the past. He was determined to lead by example, showing that no one would work any harder.

"Every time I've played, if we've come off the field after a loss, I've been able to say, 'I wish

Peyton, shown here in his rookie season, easily carried the poise and success he had in college to the pros.

I could've played better this day or had this throw back,'" Peyton once told *Football Digest*. "But I've never had to say, 'I wish I would've prepared harder.'"

The hard work quickly paid off. The next year, the Colts pulled off an amazing turnaround by reversing its 3–13 record to 13–3 and winning a

Dynamic Duo

One big reason quarterback Peyton Manning continues to set passing records is the **continuity** in the Colts' offensive system. Ever since Peyton arrived in Indianapolis in 1998, he has worked with the same offensive coordinator (Tom Moore) and the same offensive line coach (Howard Mudd). And he's had the same favorite receiver, too: Marvin Harrison (88, left).

Peyton and Marvin have worked so hard and so long together that they know what the other is going to do on the field. Sometimes, they can communicate with just a look or a nod. Other times, the quarterback knows how his wide receiver will adjust on a pass pattern because the two have been through it so many times before.

Through the 2005 season, Peyton and Marvin had teamed on 94 touchdown passes for the Colts. That's more than any other pair in NFL history. The previous record belonged to former San Francisco 49ers quarterback Steve Young and wide receiver Jerry Rice, who combined on 85 scoring tosses from 1987 to 1999.

Peyton and Colts' head coach Tony Dungy (in cap, facing camera) quickly learned that they made a perfect team.

division championship. Peyton passed for 4,135 yards and 26 touchdowns. He made the **Pro Bowl** for the first of six times over the next seven seasons.

Since then, the Colts have been consistent winners and Peyton has posted statistics that surely will land him in the Pro Football Hall of Fame once his playing career is over. He passed for more than 4,000 yards an NFL-record six seasons in a row (1999-2004), and compiled a whole list of other impressive numbers.

The most significant number, though, may have been the 49 touchdown passes that he threw in the 2004 season. That broke the 20-year-old league record of 48 set by Miami's Dan Marino. It was the equivalent of a baseball player setting a new record

Peyton posed with Dan Marino at the 2005 Pro Bowl in Hawaii after breaking Marino's single-season TD pass record.

Relief Pitchers

When Hurricane Katrina devastated the Gulf Coast region in the summer of 2005, NFL quarterbacks Peyton Manning and Eli Manning quickly volunteered to help. They donated money to help the victims of the tragedy, but they didn't stop there. Peyton, in fact, arranged for a plane to pick up supplies from his charitable foundation in Indianapolis. After helping to pack up the plane, Peyton and Eli flew in it to Louisiana and helped unpack the supplies there, too.

The Mannings grew up in New Orleans, so the tragedy was personal for them. "The whole town is like family," Peyton told CNN. "We know these people. These people know us."

for home runs in a season or a basketball player establishing a new standard for points scored.

In addition to being a prolific passer, Peyton has proven to be remarkably durable, too. Through 2005, he had been the Colts' starting quarterback for all 128 of the team's regular-season games since he joined the league. That's the most of any quarterback in NFL history from the start of a passer's career.

CHAPTER 4

One Nearly Super Season

SOMETIMES, A TRUE LEADER HAS TO SACRIFICE personal glory for the good of his team. In Peyton Manning's case, that meant throwing fewer touchdown passes and passing yards in exchange for more victories in 2005.

"I feel that I have to do my part—that for us to win, I have to play at a high level," he told *Football Digest* before the season. "Bottom line, I need to get us into the end zone. Whether that is by run or pass, it doesn't matter. Last year, we threw a lot. But if we rush for five touchdowns and win 35–7, I'm just as happy."

The Colts knew that the best way for them to win most of the time in the early 2000s was for Manning to throw for as many yards and as many touchdowns as possible. But in 2005, the team finished building the defense that it needed to balance the offense. That meant Manning's job sometimes was to slow the pace of the game, controlling the football with short tosses and runs instead of long downfield passes.

In 2005, Peyton and the Colts increased focus on the running game. Here Peyton hands off to fullback Ran Carthon.

Peyton's Big Moment

With a quarterback as successful as Peyton Manning, it's hard to find much to pick on. But his critics liked to point to four losses in a row to rival Florida while in college and seven straight defeats at New England in the pros. In 2005, though, Manning silenced those critics by leading the Colts to a 40-21 victory over the

Patriots at New England's Gillette Stadium in week 10 of the season.

The Patriots had won three of the last four Super Bowls and ended Indianapolis' season in the playoffs in 2003 and 2004. They seemed to be the only team that knew how to stop the Colts' quarterback. But in this Monday night game, Peyton shredded New England for 321 yards and three touchdown passes.

The monkey was off Peyton's back. But in typical fashion, he was more interested in the significance of the Colts' victory. "I think we are more of a team and kind of feed off each other," he said afterward. "It's definitely the best **camaraderie** we've had since I've been here eight years."

Early in the 2005 season, for instance, Indianapolis beat the Jacksonville Jaguars 10–3 and Peyton did not throw a touchdown pass. The next week, the Colts downed the Cleveland Browns 13–6, and Indianapolis scored its only touchdown on a run. Such low-scoring wins had been unheard of since Manning came along in 1998. But the key word is "wins." As long as the Colts continued winning, Peyton had no problem with how they did it.

And the wins kept on coming. A 31–10 victory over Tennessee got the offense going. A key victory over former nemesis New England improved Indianapolis to 9-0. And a 26-18 victory over Jacksonville made the Colts only the third team since the AFL-NFL merger in 1970 to begin a year with 13 wins in a row.

The Colts' dream of a perfect season ended with a loss to San Diego in the 14th game of the season. But by that time, they already had clinched a division championship and **homefield advantage** in the postseason.

In the end, Indianapolis won 14 games during the regular season. It was the most in more than 50 years of franchise history. Peyton still ended up with

In 1970, the ten-year-old American Football League merge with the National Football League, which had been founded in 1920. The combined league divided into the American and National Football Conferences.

statistics that ranked among the best in the NFL: 3,747 yards and 28 touchdown passes.

Manning has become one of the top quarterbacks not just in the NFL today, but perhaps in league history. While he continues to lead the Colts on the field, and to try to follow his father's example off the field, he'll also continue to look for just one more thing to make his career perfect: a Super Bowl championship.

A familiar sight—Manning celebrating another Colts' touchdown pass. He has nearly 250 in his first eight seasons.

Peyton Manning's Career Statistics

Year	G-GS	Att.	Comp.	Pct.	Yds	TD	Int	Long	Rating
1998	16-16	575	326	56.7	3,739	26	28	78	71.2
1999	16-16	533	331	62.1	4,135	26	15	80	90.7
2000	16-16	571	357	62.5	4,413	33	15	78	94.7
2001	16-16	547	343	62.7	4,131	26	23	86	84.1
2002	16-16	591	392	66.3	4,200	27	19	69	88.8
2003	16-16	566	379	67.0	4,267	29	10	79	99.0
2004	16-16	497	336	67.6	4,557	49	10	80	121.1
2005	16-16	453	305	67.3	3,747	28	10	80	104.1
Career	128-128	4,333	2,769	63.9	33,189	244	130	86	93.5

LEGEND: G-GS: games played/games started; Att.: attempts; Comp.: completions; Pct.: completion percentage; Yds: passing yards; TD: touchdown passes; Int: interceptions; Long: longest completed pass; Rating: passer rating, a stat that combines several numbers to create a figure that compares NFL quarterbacks' success.

GLOSSARY

amateur a person who is not paid for his or her skill or art (in this case, to play sports)

camaraderie the feeling of getting along well together, usually among friends

continuity a continuous flow, or unbroken duration

cum laude a Latin phrase meaning, "with honors"

ecstatic very excited

eligibility meeting all rules that let you take part in sports

exhorting urging, admonishing, encouraging

homefield advantage the benefit a team gets from playing in its home stadium

hype attention paid to a person or story in the media that inflates what is expected of that person or story

Pro Bowl the NFL's annual all-star game, played between the best players from teams in the American Football Conference (AFC) against the best players from teams in the National Football Conference (NFC)

BOOKS

Peyton Manning
> By *Geoffrey M. Horn*
> (Gareth Stevens Publishing, Milwaukee) 2005
> A complete biography of the Colts' superstar, including how he learned from his father.

Peyton Manning: Indianapolis Colts Star Quarterback
> By *Joanne Mattern*
> (Mitchell Lane Publishers, Delaware) 2006
> This book is a biography of the Indianapolis Colts' quarterback, whose father was also a professional quarterback.

Peyton Manning: Passing the Record
> By *Indy-Tech Publishing*
> (Sams Technical Publishing, Indianapolis) 2005
> This book focuses on the 2004 NFL season, which saw Manning break the single-season touchdown passing record.

Peyton Manning: Primed and Ready
> By *Jimmy Hyams*
> (Addax Publishing Group, Kansas) 1998
> This book gives an in-depth look at Manning's college career at Tennessee, and provides insights into his thoughts on not winning the Heisman Trophy.

WEB SITES

Visit our home page for lots of links about Peyton Manning:
www.childsworld.com/links

Note to Parents, Teachers, and Librarians: We routinely check our Web links to make sure they're safe, active sites—so encourage your readers to check them out!

INDEX

ABOUT THE AUTHOR

Jim Gigliotti is a writer who lives in southern California with his wife and two children. A former editor with the National Football League's publishing division, he has written more than a dozen books about sports and personalities, including *Stadium Stories: USC Trojans* and *Watching Football* (with former NFL star Daryl Johnston).